Eye On The Environment

OIL SPILLS

J.M. Patten, Ed.D.

The Rourke Book Co., Inc.
Vero Beach, Florida 32964

Edited by Pamela J.P. Schroeder and Sandra A. Robinson

PHOTO CREDITS
Courtesy of U.S. Fish and Wildlife Service: cover; courtesy of Alaska Center for the Environment: pages 4, 9, 10, 13, 15, 16, 18, 19, 21, 22; courtesy of Alaska Commission on the Environment: page 6; © J.M. Patten: page 7

Library of Congress Cataloging-in-Publication Data

Patten, J.M., 1944-
    Oil spills / J.M. Patten.
    p. cm. — (Eye on the environment)
    Includes index.
    ISBN 1-55916-096-9
    1. Oil spills—Environmental aspects—Juvenile literature.
[1. Oil spills. 2. Water—Pollution. 3. Pollution.] I. Title. II. Series.
TD196.P4.P4P38   1995
363.73'82—dc20   94-37162
                                                                CIP
                                                                AC

Printed in the USA

TABLE OF CONTENTS

EYE ON OIL SPILLS

This book is about oil spills. You will find out how oil spills happen and how they harm the Earth's **environment.**

The Earth's environment is all living and nonliving things in the world. The soil we farm, air we breathe, and water we drink are important parts of the environment. People must work to keep the environment clean and safe.

Earth is our home—the only known place where people, plants and animals can live. Oil spills damage our home, hurting us all.

Bright sunlight reflects off a huge and deadly oil spill near the Alaska coast.

OIL IS SPECIAL

Oil is a **natural resource,** something not made by people. It comes from wells drilled deep in the ground. People use oil to make many useful things.

Workers watch a spinning drill on an oil drilling platform.

Many power stations use oil to make the electricity we need to heat and light our homes and stores.

Gasoline and other fuels come from oil. Almost every car, truck, bus, train and ship runs on fuel made from oil.

People use oil to make some medicines—and even clothes. Toys, paints, plastic bottles, garbage bags and many car parts are made from oil, too.

DANGER FROM OIL

Oil, used carefully, helps people. When oil spills into rivers and oceans, it **pollutes,** or poisons, part of our environment.

Oil spilled on water doesn't sink. Oil is lighter than water, and floats like a cork. Greasy, green-black oil stays on top of the water, and the winds and tides spread it around.

Spilled oil can be very thick and feels sticky, like hot fudge. Floating oil can cover the ocean and smear the shoreline for miles.

The long neck of an oil-killed bird (front) stretches out of a thick, sticky oil spill along a sandy beach.

OIL SPILLED ON WATER

Some oil leaks and spills onto water by accident. Oil **tankers,** ships that carry oil, can hit rocks and break open. Leaking tankers may spill tons of oil onto the water before help arrives. Sometimes, people who don't care about the environment pump oil out of the ships into oceans, lakes and rivers.

Oil is spilled on land, too. Rain can wash this oil into the water. Scientists say 7 million tons of oil pollute ocean water every year.

This dark ribbon of leaking oil floats beside a harbor work boat.

WHEN OIL WASHES ASHORE

Oil spills that come ashore wash over the sand and rocks. The beach becomes coated with sticky, dangerous oil. Oil on the beach covers the **habitat,** or homes, of sea life.

Birds covered with oil have no chance of survival without human help.

This special oil cleanup barge sprays shoreline rocks with water to remove oil.

Clams, mussels, snails and crabs soak in oil and die. Many shoreline plants, tiny eggs and fish die, too.

Oil hurts our water environment. However, people can prevent oil spills if they handle oil carefully.

SEA BIRDS AND OIL SPILLS

Oil spills kill many birds. Most sea birds cannot survive in water polluted with oil.

Diving, wading and swimming birds become helpless in oil spills. Oil covers their beaks, eyes and feathers. They cannot fly or swim out of the oil.

In large oil spills, thousands of sea birds may die. **Veterinarians,** or animal doctors, and trained volunteers try to save as many as they can.

This frightened bird hopes that people can clean the oil from its beak and feathers.

SEA OTTERS AND OIL SPILLS

Sea otters are ocean animals. They live near shore in **herds,** or groups, and almost never leave the water.

Sea otters dive deep into very cold water for their favorite foods. Their fluffy fur traps air and keeps sea otters warm.

Oil in the water soaks the otters' fur. Oil mats the fur so it sticks to their skin and can't keep them warm. Many sea otters freeze when spilled oil pollutes their environment.

The oil-soaked fur of this sea otter must be cleaned or the animal will freeze in cold water.

OIL SPILL CLEANUP AT SEA

When oil spills from a ship at sea, trained workers and scientists rush to help. They follow emergency plans they made before the spill even happened.

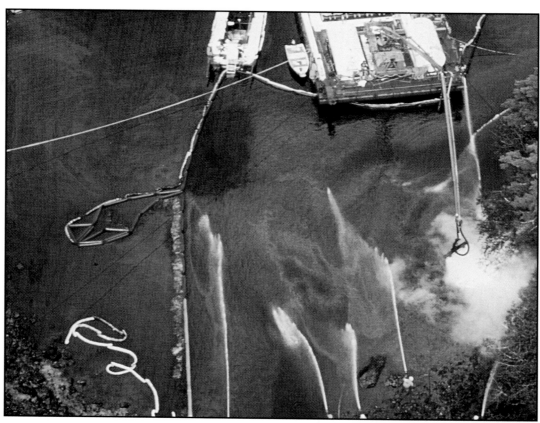

Workers hose oil off the land and into the water toward a "boom," which traps the oil so it can be sucked up by rescue ships.

Powerful streams of water clean oil from rocks along the Alaska shoreline.

Workers quickly pump oil from the leaking tanker into rescue ships. They keep tons of oil from spilling into the ocean this way.

Rescue workers surround the oil that gets onto the water with a "boom"—a long, air-filled tube that looks like a floating fire hose. Oil is held in one place so it can't spread easily. The workers pump the trapped oil off the water into waiting ships.

OIL CLEANUP ON SHORE

Spilled oil sometimes pollutes the shore. When this happens, trained workers and scientists spring into action.

Workers use hoses to wash oil off rocks. In some places, they pick up stones and clean them by hand. Scientists and volunteers gently wash oiled birds and animals with mild soap and release them into clean water.

After the cleanup work is done, plants, birds and animals start to move back to the places once polluted by oil. Scientists and volunteers check often to make sure the environment is safe.

This tired cleanup crew has the difficult job of cleaning the spilled oil from shoreline rocks.

GLOSSARY

environment (en VI ren ment) — the world around us including plants, animals, soil, water and air

habitat (HAB uh tat) — homes

herd (HERD) — a group of animals

natural resource (NA chur uhl REE sors) — useful things that are not made by people

pollute (puh LOOT) — to poison

tanker (TANK er) — a ship that carries oil

veterinarian (vet er in AIR ee un) — a doctor for animals

This captive bald eagle awaits a medical checkup by volunteer animal doctors at the site of an oil spill.

INDEX